FOOD LOVER'S
~ Recipe ~
NOTEBOOK

EBURY PRESS STATIONERY

First published in 1991 by Ebury Press Stationery
An imprint of the Random Century Group
Random Century House, 20 Vauxhall Bridge Road,
London SW1V 2SA

Set in Palatino
by FMT Graphics Limited, Southwark, London

Printed in Hong Kong
Designed by Grahame Dudley

Picture research by Gabrielle Allen

ISBN 0 7126 45284

Front cover illustration: **Still Life** Joris Van Son
Back cover illustration: **Fruit** Thomas F. Collier

FOOD LOVER'S
Recipe
NOTEBOOK

ℰℬ

EBURY PRESS STATIONERY

Soups and Starters

Recipe for

Ingredients

Method

Comments

RECIPE FOR

INGREDIENTS

METHOD

COMMENTS

RECIPE FOR

INGREDIENTS

METHOD

COMMENTS

RECIPE FOR

INGREDIENTS

METHOD

COMMENTS

RECIPE FOR

INGREDIENTS

METHOD

COMMENTS

RECIPE FOR

INGREDIENTS

METHOD

COMMENTS

RECIPE FOR

INGREDIENTS

METHOD

COMMENTS

RECIPE FOR

INGREDIENTS

METHOD

COMMENTS

RECIPE FOR

INGREDIENTS

METHOD

COMMENTS

Fish and Shellfish

Recipe for

Ingredients

Method

Comments

RECIPE FOR

INGREDIENTS

METHOD

COMMENTS

RECIPE FOR

INGREDIENTS

METHOD

COMMENTS

Recipe for

Ingredients

Method

Comments

RECIPE FOR

INGREDIENTS

METHOD

COMMENTS

RECIPE FOR

INGREDIENTS

METHOD

COMMENTS

RECIPE FOR

INGREDIENTS

METHOD

COMMENTS

RECIPE FOR

INGREDIENTS

METHOD

COMMENTS

RECIPE FOR

INGREDIENTS

METHOD

COMMENTS

Meat, Poultry and Game

RECIPE FOR

INGREDIENTS

METHOD

COMMENTS

Recipe for

Ingredients

Method

Comments

RECIPE FOR

INGREDIENTS

METHOD

COMMENTS

RECIPE FOR

INGREDIENTS

METHOD

COMMENTS

RECIPE FOR

INGREDIENTS

METHOD

COMMENTS

RECIPE FOR

INGREDIENTS

METHOD

COMMENTS

RECIPE FOR

INGREDIENTS

METHOD

COMMENTS

RECIPE FOR

INGREDIENTS

METHOD

COMMENTS

RECIPE FOR

INGREDIENTS

METHOD

COMMENTS

RECIPE FOR

INGREDIENTS

METHOD

COMMENTS

RECIPE FOR

INGREDIENTS

METHOD

COMMENTS

Salads, Vegetables and Side Dishes

RECIPE FOR

INGREDIENTS

METHOD

COMMENTS

RECIPE FOR

INGREDIENTS

METHOD

COMMENTS

RECIPE FOR

INGREDIENTS

METHOD

COMMENTS

RECIPE FOR

INGREDIENTS

METHOD

COMMENTS

RECIPE FOR

INGREDIENTS

METHOD

COMMENTS

RECIPE FOR

INGREDIENTS

METHOD

COMMENTS

RECIPE FOR

INGREDIENTS

METHOD

COMMENTS

RECIPE FOR

INGREDIENTS

METHOD

COMMENTS

RECIPE FOR

INGREDIENTS

METHOD

COMMENTS

RECIPE FOR

INGREDIENTS

METHOD

COMMENTS

RECIPE FOR

INGREDIENTS

METHOD

COMMENTS

Eggs, Cheese and Vegetarian Dishes

RECIPE FOR

INGREDIENTS

METHOD

COMMENTS

RECIPE FOR

INGREDIENTS

METHOD

COMMENTS

RECIPE FOR

INGREDIENTS

METHOD

COMMENTS

RECIPE FOR

INGREDIENTS

METHOD

COMMENTS

RECIPE FOR

INGREDIENTS

METHOD

COMMENTS

RECIPE FOR

INGREDIENTS

METHOD

COMMENTS

RECIPE FOR

INGREDIENTS

METHOD

COMMENTS

RECIPE FOR

INGREDIENTS

METHOD

COMMENTS

RECIPE FOR

INGREDIENTS

METHOD

COMMENTS

Recipe for

Ingredients

Method

Comments

RECIPE FOR

INGREDIENTS

METHOD

COMMENTS

Desserts

Recipe for

Ingredients

Method

Comments

RECIPE FOR

INGREDIENTS

METHOD

COMMENTS

RECIPE FOR

INGREDIENTS

METHOD

COMMENTS

RECIPE FOR

INGREDIENTS

METHOD

COMMENTS

RECIPE FOR

INGREDIENTS

METHOD

COMMENTS

RECIPE FOR

INGREDIENTS

METHOD

COMMENTS

RECIPE FOR

INGREDIENTS

METHOD

COMMENTS

RECIPE FOR

INGREDIENTS

METHOD

COMMENTS

RECIPE FOR

INGREDIENTS

METHOD

COMMENTS

RECIPE FOR

INGREDIENTS

METHOD

COMMENTS

RECIPE FOR

INGREDIENTS

METHOD

COMMENTS

RECIPE FOR

INGREDIENTS

METHOD

COMMENTS

RECIPE FOR

INGREDIENTS

METHOD

COMMENTS

BAKING

RECIPE FOR

INGREDIENTS

METHOD

COMMENTS

RECIPE FOR

INGREDIENTS

METHOD

COMMENTS

RECIPE FOR

INGREDIENTS

METHOD

COMMENTS

RECIPE FOR

INGREDIENTS

METHOD

COMMENTS

RECIPE FOR

INGREDIENTS

METHOD

COMMENTS

RECIPE FOR

INGREDIENTS

METHOD

COMMENTS

Baking

RECIPE FOR

INGREDIENTS

METHOD

COMMENTS

RECIPE FOR

INGREDIENTS

METHOD

COMMENTS

RECIPE FOR

INGREDIENTS

METHOD

COMMENTS

RECIPE FOR

INGREDIENTS

METHOD

COMMENTS

RECIPE FOR

INGREDIENTS

METHOD

COMMENTS

SUPPLIERS

BOUCHERIE

PICTURE CREDITS

Soups and Starters:
Making Soup, C. V. M. Desliens. Fine Art
Photographic Library Ltd.

Fish and Shellfish:
A Still Life with Crab, Lobster and Oysters, Abraham
Hendricksz van Beyeren (1620-1675), Fine Art
Photographic Library Ltd.

Meat, Poultry and Game:
Truffled Paté, Maerten Boelema de Stomme (c. 1642),
Musee des Beaux-Arts, Nantes.
The Bridgeman Art Library.

Salads, Vegetables and Side Dishes:
Vegetable Market, Lucas van Valkenborch (1530-97)
Kunsthistorisches Museum, Vienna.
The Bridgeman Art Library.

Eggs, Cheese and Vegetarian Dishes:
Still Life with Bread and Cheese, Floris van Schooten
(c. 1612), Harold Samuel Collection, Corporation
of London. The Bridgeman Art Library.

Desserts:
Plums, Grapes and Raspberries in a Porcelain Tureen,
Sophus Pedersen. Christie's Colour Library.

Baking:
The Maid with the Milk Jug, Jan Vermeer (1632-1675),
Rijksmuseum, Amsterdam.
The Bridgeman Art Library.

Suppliers:
The Marketplace, (1885), Victor Gabriel Gilbert
(1847-1933). Fine Art Photographic Library Ltd.